MADE IN MEXICO

PETER LAUFER

SUSAN L. ROTH

NATIONAL GEOGRAPHIC SOCIETY
WASHINGTON, D.C.

PRODUCTOS PARA MADERA
SELLADORES,
LACAS,
BRILLO DIRECTO,
TINTES,
TAPA POROS,
THINNE

MONEY ORDER AMERICAN EXPRESS
CHEQUE DE VIAJERO TRAVELERS EXPRESS

In Mexico, everybody loves the typical mariachis, who stroll the streets wearing their wide-brimmed sombreros, singing songs of love and adventure. Mariachis play requintos and bass violins, guitarrones and mandolinas. And they play guitars.

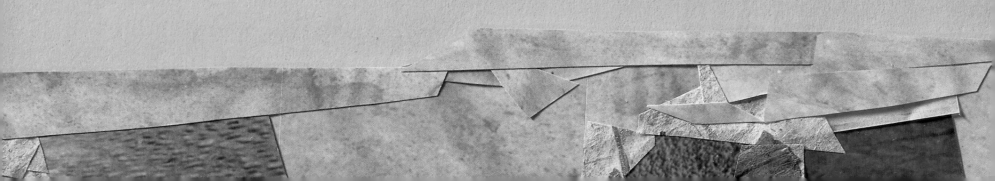

From Chihuahua in the north to Oaxaca in the south, from the Atlántico to the Pacífico, mariachis know that the best guitars in Mexico come from a little village in the Michoacán mountains called Paracho.

But there's more than mariachi music in Mexico.

In the Zona Rosa in Mexico City, guitarristas play jazz in the smoky nightclubs on guitars made in Paracho.

Sí, there's more than mariachi music in Mexico.

In concert halls all around Mexico,
musicians sit alone on formal stages
with their guitars, performing the classics.

Sí, hay más que música de mariachis en México.

For many years these classical musicians chose guitars made in Spain, the U.S.A., and Japan because they considered them the best instruments they could find in all the world. But recently, some guitar makers in Paracho are surprising guitarists with something new—concert guitars that look and sound just as good as any made anywhere else.

Now, even more than mariachi guitars are made in Mexico.

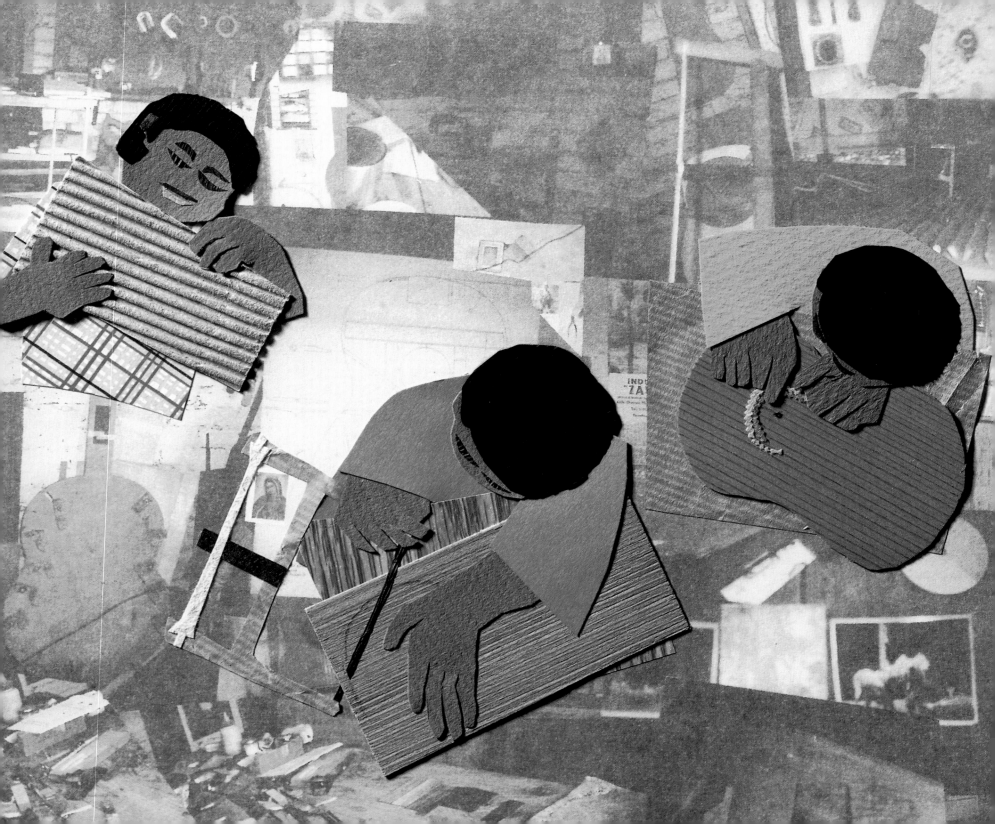

In workshops on the side streets of Paracho, experienced guitar makers use hand saws and homemade knives to shape mostly Mexican woods into guitar parts. Slowly and carefully they cut and saw, glue and sand. Finally, they varnish and polish. Building a fine concert quality guitar takes at least a month of work.

Sí, más que guitarras para mariachis se hacen en México.

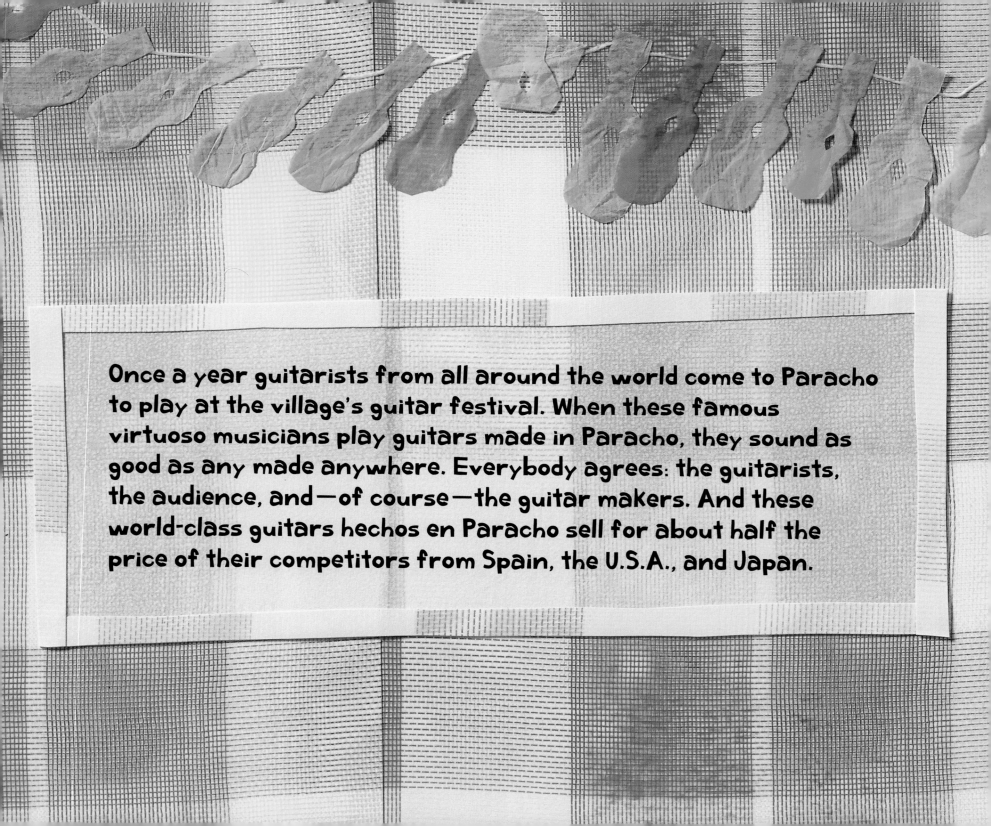

Once a year guitarists from all around the world come to Paracho to play at the village's guitar festival. When these famous virtuoso musicians play guitars made in Paracho, they sound as good as any made anywhere. Everybody agrees: the guitarists, the audience, and—of course—the guitar makers. And these world-class guitars hechos en Paracho sell for about half the price of their competitors from Spain, the U.S.A., and Japan.

Por Tradición... GUITARREROS PARACHO

The U.S.A.-Mexico border crossing at San Diego and Tijuana is the busiest border in the world. Tourists from California and all the States flock south for sun and fun in Mexico. These norteamericanos find fun and sun. And they find poverty and desperation.

Immediately south of the border, little children—with dirty faces and ragged clothing—push at the tourists, begging, trying to sell chewing gum or cheap trinkets. There's garbage in the streets; the buildings need paint. Mexico is a poor country compared with its northern neighbor.

There's more than mariachi music in Mexico.

But deep inside Mexico, far south of the border in Paracho, the marketplace is full of fresh fruits and vegetables, fish and meat. The little children are well scrubbed and well fed. And along with reading and arithmetic, they learn about guitars.

Some learn how to build guitars—helping in the little workshops or watching in the big factories. Others learn how to sell guitars alongside their parents in the shops that line Paracho's main street.

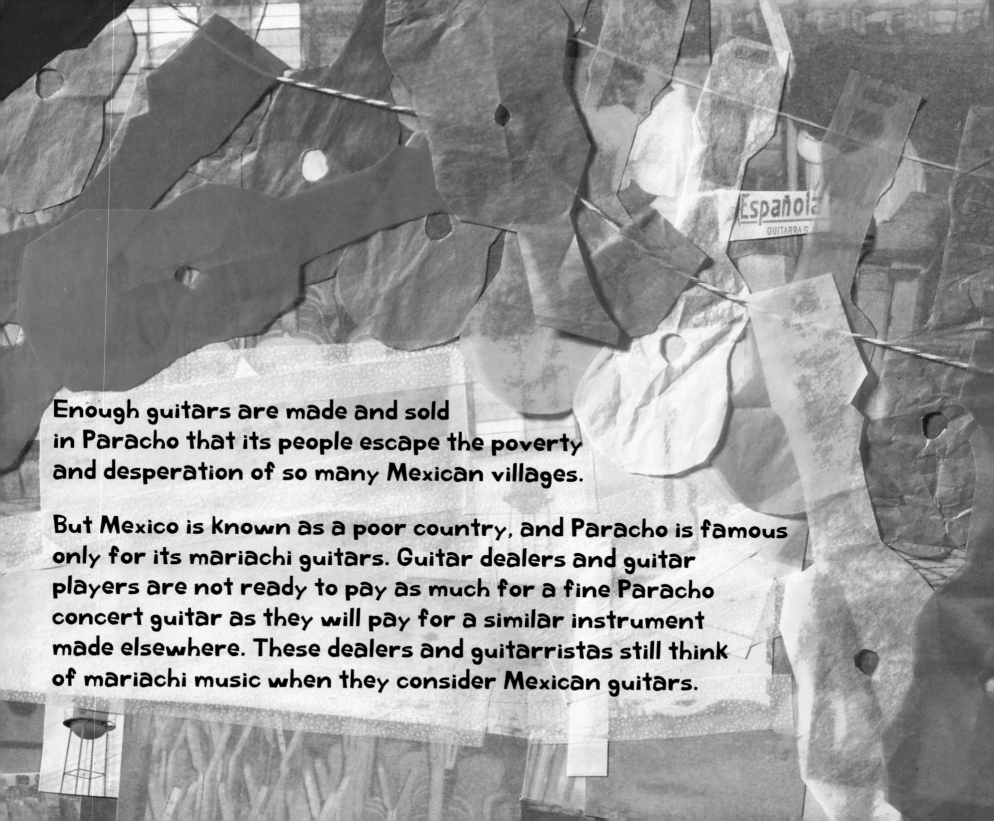

Enough guitars are made and sold
in Paracho that its people escape the poverty
and desperation of so many Mexican villages.

But Mexico is known as a poor country, and Paracho is famous
only for its mariachi guitars. Guitar dealers and guitar
players are not ready to pay as much for a fine Paracho
concert guitar as they will pay for a similar instrument
made elsewhere. These dealers and guitarristas still think
of mariachi music when they consider Mexican guitars.

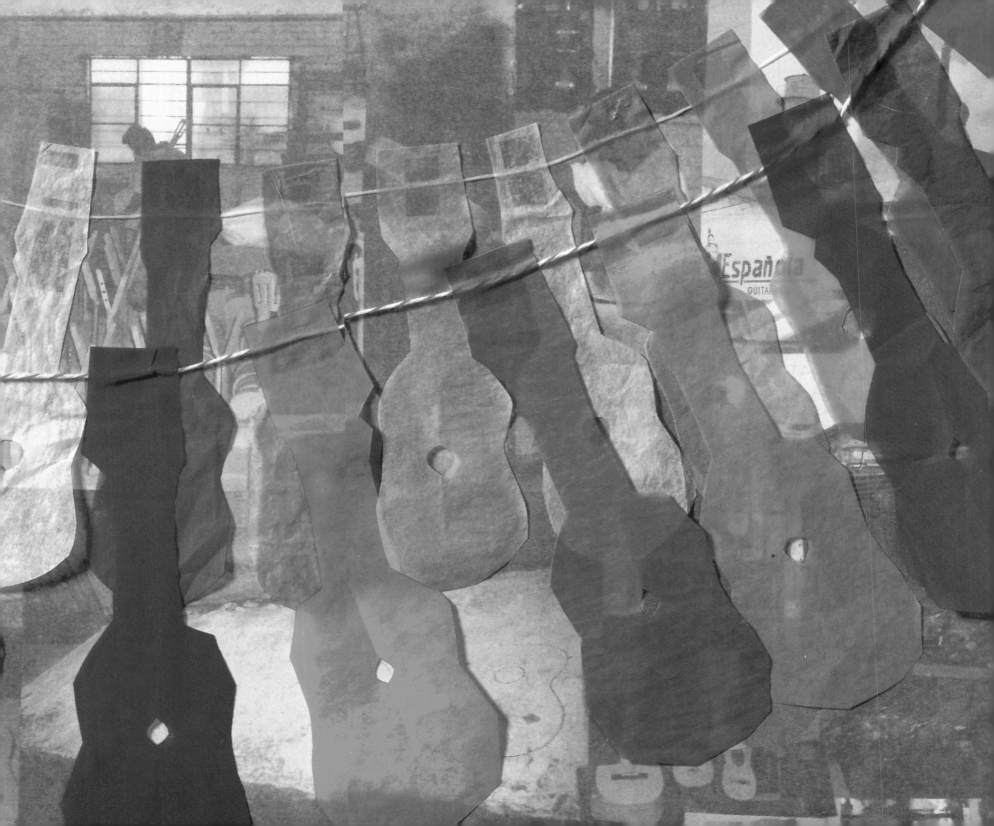

Paracho's fine guitar makers are patient, confident that soon the rest of the world will also realize...

...que hay más que música de mariachis en México.
There's more than mariachi music in Mexico.

Author's Note

I first encountered Paracho when my son Talmage, who is a guitarist, showed me a guitar he bought from a mariachi musician. As we looked over the instrument, we were puzzled by the label, which located the maker's shop in "Paracho, Mich." We were quite sure the guitar was not from some village in Michigan. We dragged out the atlas and found tiny Paracho, situated in the state of Michoacán, about midpoint between Mexico City and Guadalajara. A few months later we pooled my frequent flyer points and took off on a whim: Tal wanted to tour the shop that had made his guitar. A few days later we finally bounced into Paracho in a rickety old bus and discovered for ourselves the magic of this special village.

There are many stories about how Paracho became the most important place in Mexico for guitars. Some people say that during colonial times a Spanish priest decided to choose useful trades to teach the poor villagers of Michoacán. He taught some villages furniture making and pottery, others copper work and weaving. Father Juan de San Miguel picked guitar making for Paracho. Other stories suggest Paracho ended up a guitar center simply by chance.

Whatever the true story, today guitars fill every store in Paracho. The workshops of instrument makers are tucked away on side streets and alleys. The big guitar-building factories lie on the edge of the village. Strolling mariachis entertain shoppers in the crowded marketplace, playing guitars made in Paracho.

Every summer there is a guitar festival in Paracho. Expert guitar players and expert guitar makers gather in the little village from all over the world for concerts, to teach master classes, and to exchange guitar-making ideas and techniques. The village fills with music, and the main square is full of visitors.

Daily life in Paracho depends on the guitar, and so does Paracho's soul. The children of Paracho line up to study guitar at the village music school. There they learn not only to play their instruments but also to appreciate the importance of the guitar to their isolated mountain valley.

Susan L. Roth's collages were constructed with papers made in both Mexico and the U.S.A., photographs by Peter Laufer and Susan L. Roth, ribbons and strings, Paracho festival confetti, souvenirs, typical Mexican shopping bags and tablecloths, and real wood shavings from what are now master-crafted guitars with homes all over the world.

A hearty thanks y muchas gracias to:

At the Library of Congress: Jon Newsom, chief of the Music Division; Sybille A. Jagusch, chief of the Children's Literature Center; Georgette M. Dorn, chief of the Hispanic Division; Anne McLean, Music Specialist in charge of concerts • Jim Weaver, chief of the Music Division at the Smithsonian Institution • Alejandro C. Cervantes, founding instructor at CIDEG, the Center for the Investigation and the Development of the Guitar, in Paracho and Executive Director of the Paracho Project • Jaime Gomez, instructor at CIDEG, and his family • Carlos Monroy of Guitarras y Artesanias in Paracho • Abel Garcia, Carlos Piña, and all of the other Paracho guitar makers who opened their workshops to us • Talmage Morris, Music Director of the Paracho Project • Susan Pedersen and Beverly Maiorana at Minuteman Press in Great Neck, New York • Víctor Reyes, translator • Nina Hoffman, Nancy Feresten, and the production team at the National Geographic Society Book Division • Ann Finnell • Alana Roth • Sheila Swan Laufer • Michael Laufer

The text is set in a face designed by Susan L. Roth and Robert Salazar, and was handcut by SLR.
The book was printed and bound by Impresora Donneco Internacional, SA de C.V. in Ciudad Reynosa, Tamaulipas, Mexico

The world's largest nonprofit scientific and educational organization, the National Geographic Society was founded in 1888 "for the increase and diffusion of geographic knowledge." Since then it has supported scientific exploration and spread information to its more than nine million members worldwide. The National Geographic Society educates and inspires millions every day through magazines, books, television programs, videos, maps and atlases, research grants, the National Geography Bee, teacher workshops, and innovative classroom materials. The Society is supported through membership dues and income from the sale of its educational products. Members receive NATIONAL GEOGRAPHIC magazine—the Society's official journal—discounts on Society products, and other benefits. For more information about the National Geographic Society and its educational programs and publications, please call 1-800-NGS-LINE (647-5463) or write to the following address: National Geographic Society, 1145 17th Street N.W., Washington, D.C. 20036-4688 U.S.A. Visit the Society's Web site: www.nationalgeographic.com

Library of Congress Cataloging-in-Publication Data. Laufer, Peter. Made in Mexico / by Peter Laufer; illustrated by Susan L. Roth.
p. cm. SUMMARY: Describes the importance of the guitar in Mexico, especially in Paracho, a town which is becoming the center of the Mexican guitar industry. ISBN 0-7922-7118-1 1. Guitar – Construction – Mexico – Paracho de Verduzco Juvenile literature.
[1. Guitar. 2. Mexico – Social life and customs.] I. Roth, Susan L. ill. II. Title ML1015.G9 L38 2000 787.87'197237 – dc21
99-38220 Printed in Mexico First edition